On the farm

Written by Ruth Thomson
Illustrated by Anne Moorse

PUBLISHED BY THE READER'S DIGEST ASSOCIATION LIMITED

Ian, Mary, Mummy and Daddy were on their way to Hillside farm.

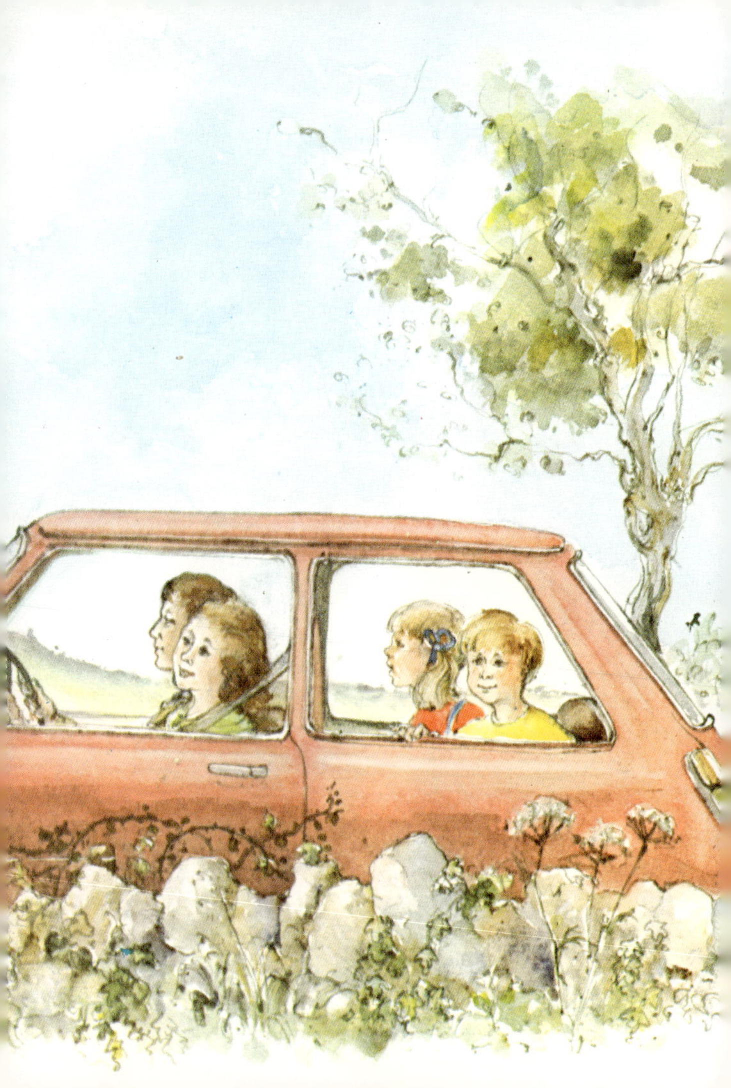

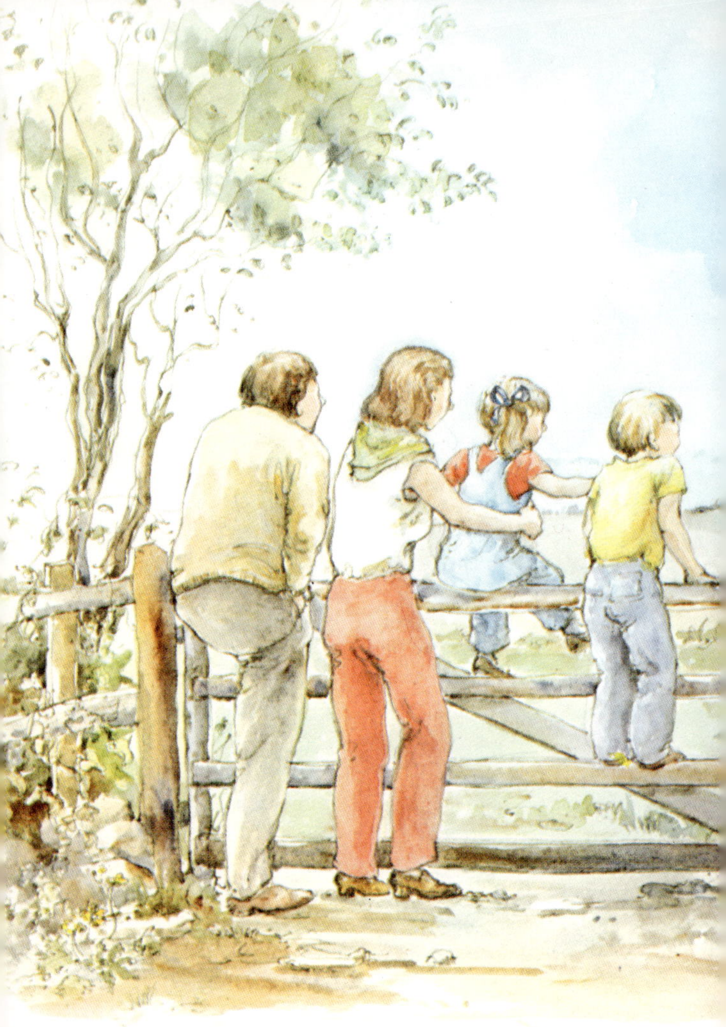

"Nearly there," said Daddy,
as they reached the top of a hill.
They all got out to look
at the farm below.

As they drove up to the farm,
Mrs Benn, Ian and Mary's aunt,
came hurrying up to meet them.

"Oh, I'm so glad you've come,"
she said. "We're so busy today,
we could do with some extra hands.
Let me show you round."

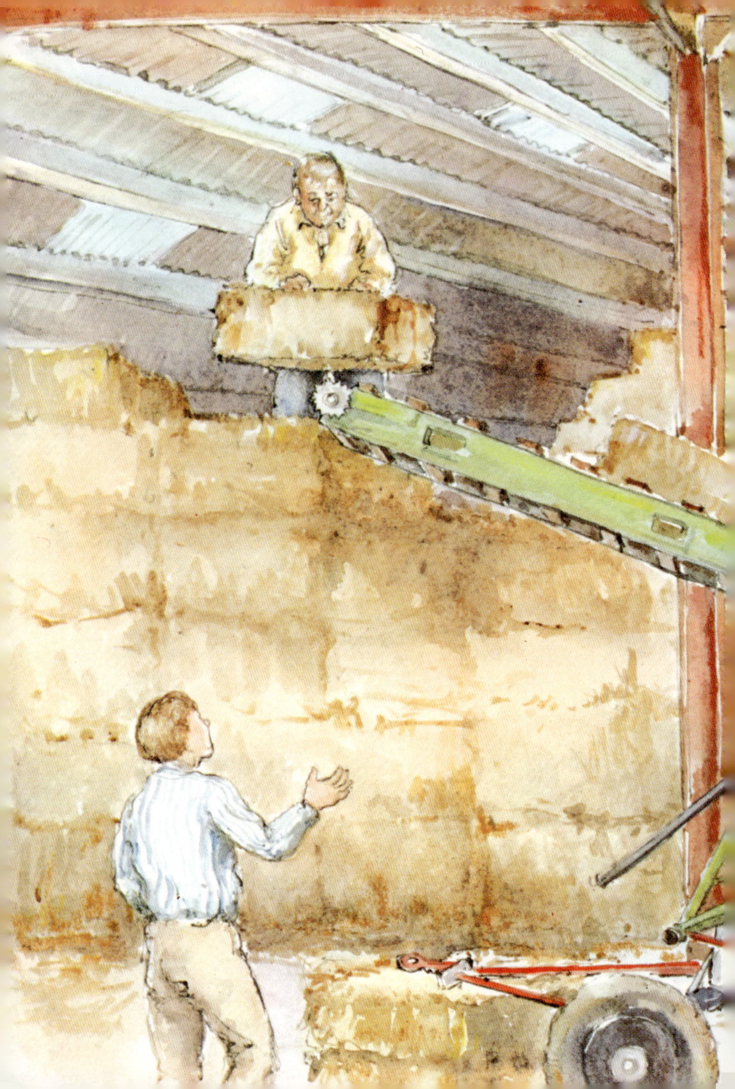

Mr Benn and Alf were stacking the hay.
Daddy offered to give them a hand.

Charlotte was milking the cows.
Mummy said she would stay and watch.

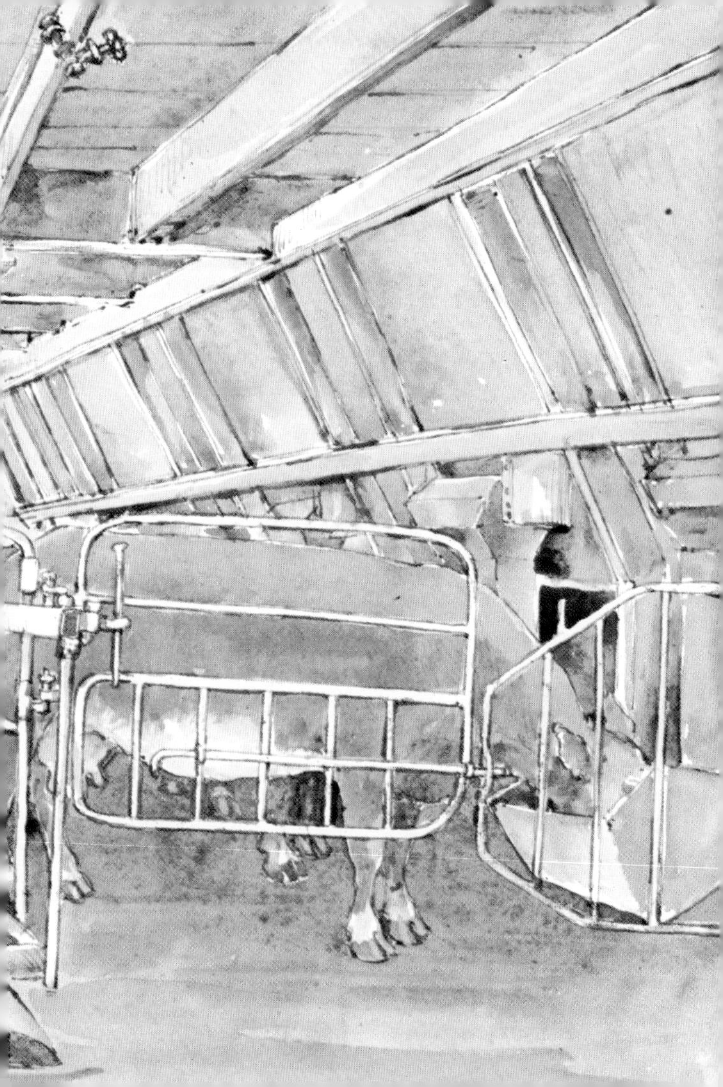

That just left Ian and Mary.
Greg was mending the tractor.

Ian and Mary watched him,
but they didn't know how to help.

"I've got two jobs for you,"
Mrs Benn said to them.
"Can you collect some eggs
and then see if you can find
our cat Suzie?
We haven't seen her for days."

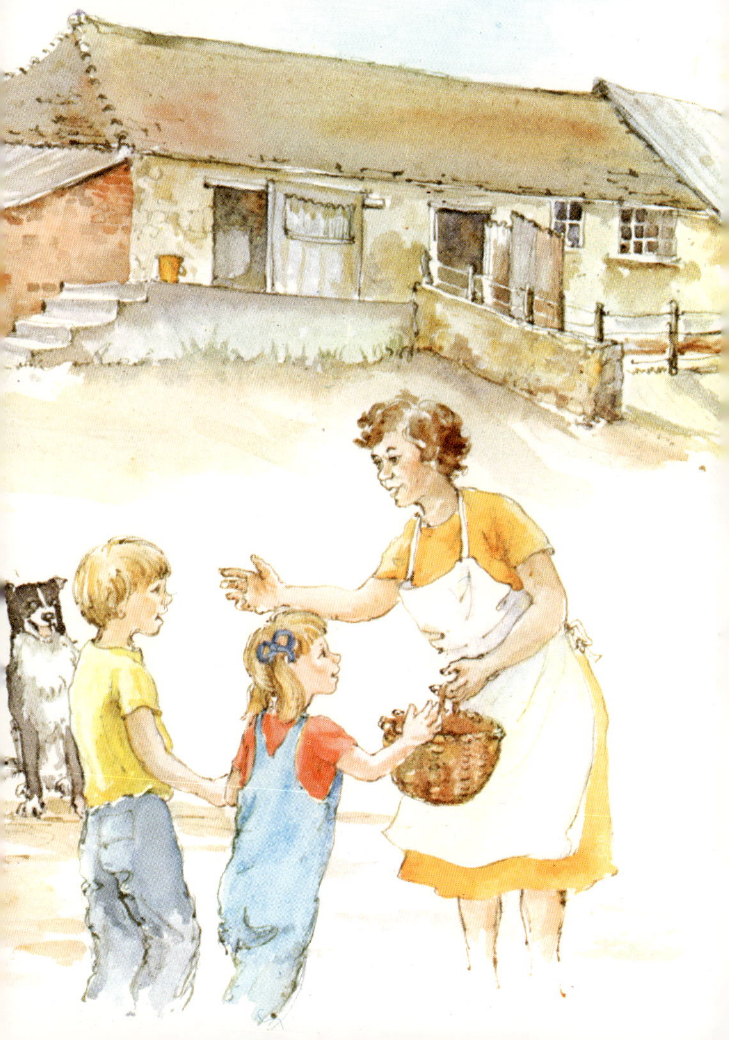

She told them where to find the hens
and off they went to get the eggs.

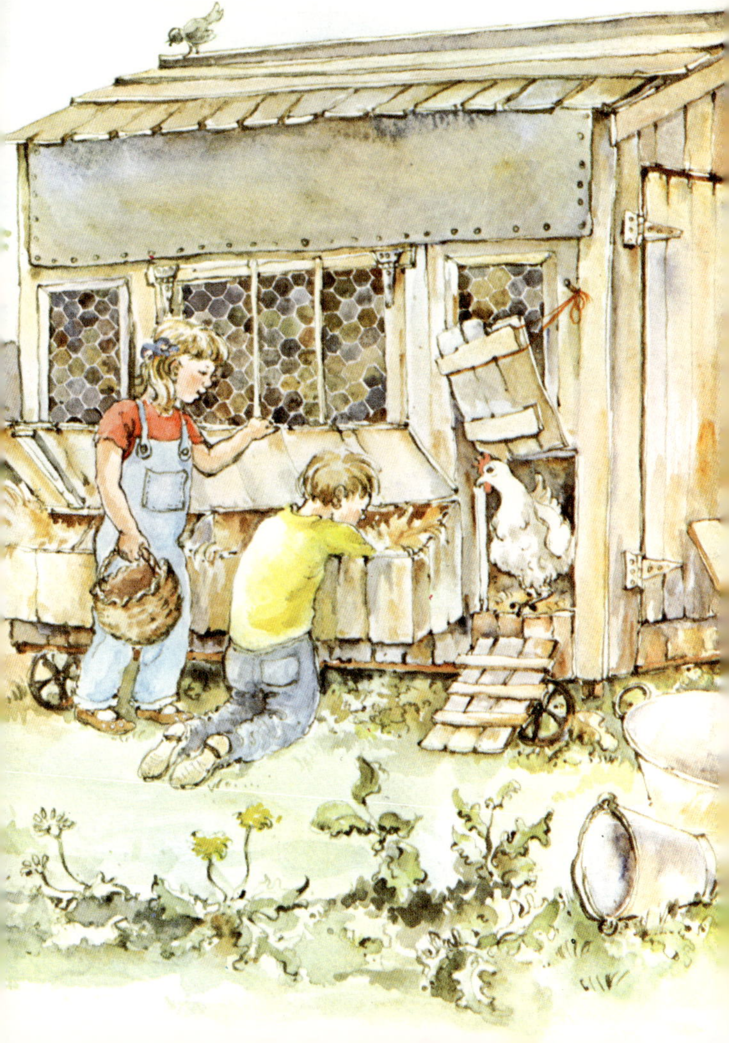

Ian and Mary were so keen
to collect the eggs,
they quite forgot to shut
the door of the chicken run.

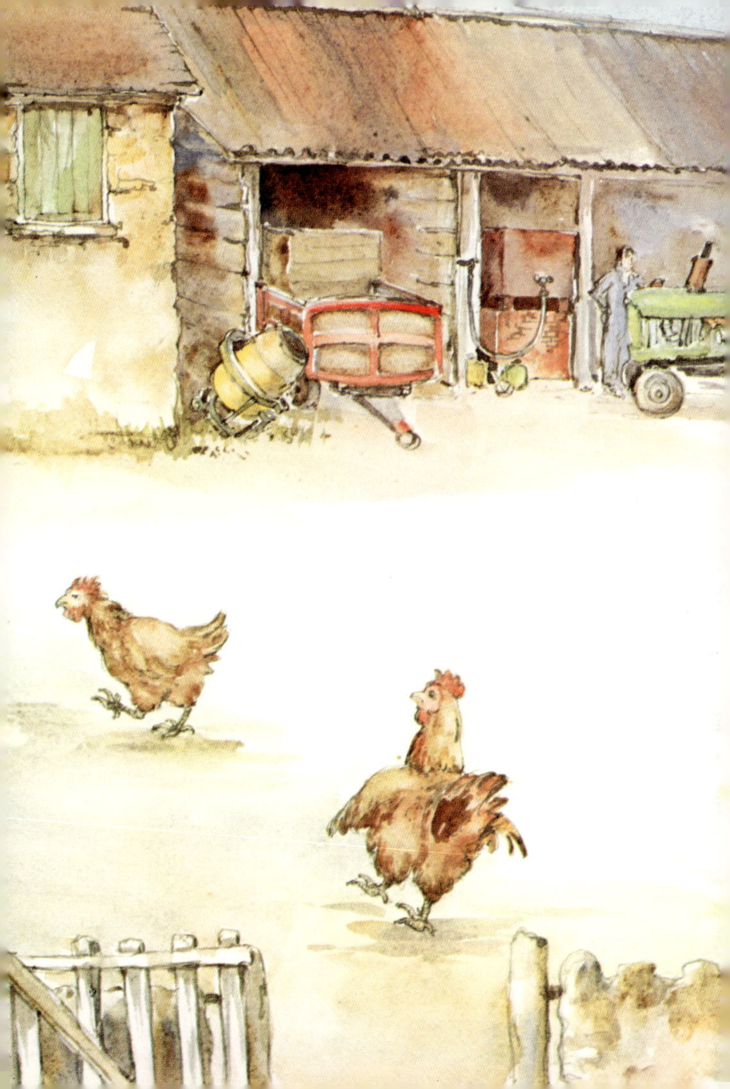

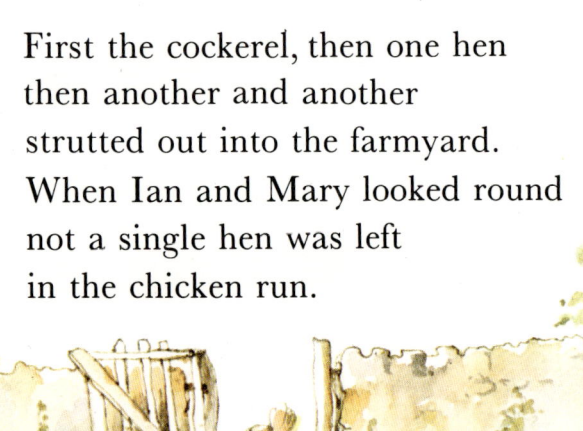

First the cockerel, then one hen
then another and another
strutted out into the farmyard.
When Ian and Mary looked round
not a single hen was left
in the chicken run.

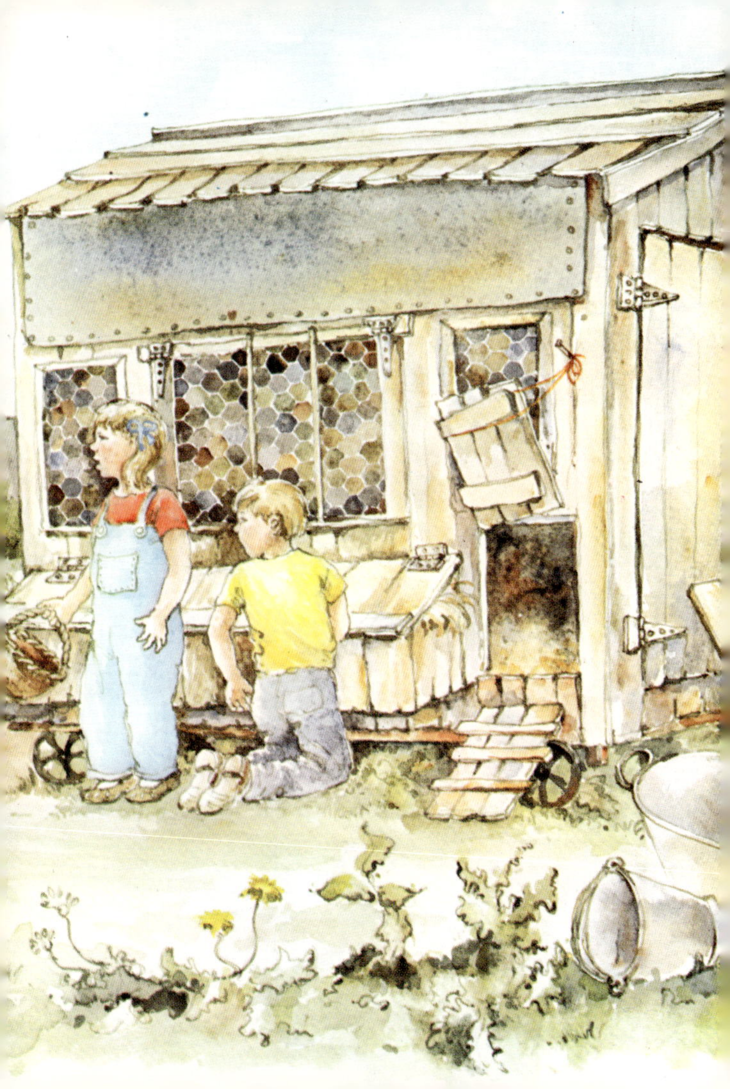

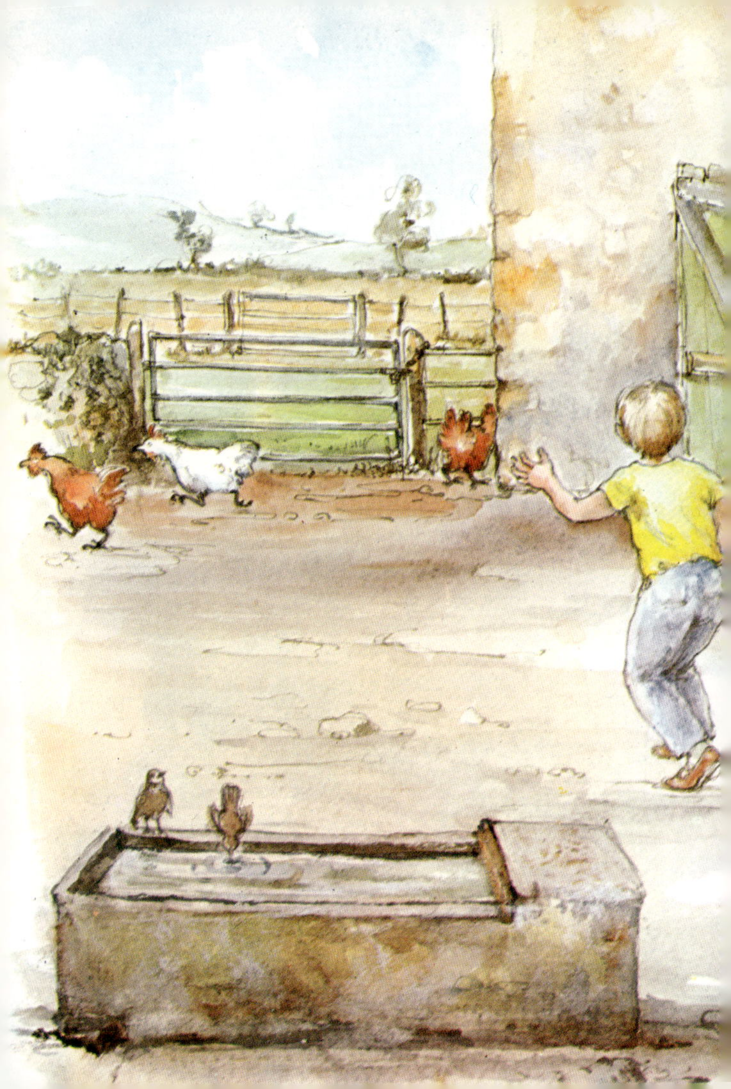

"Quick, after them!" shouted Ian,
and ran after a hen.
But it got away
around a corner.

Mary ran after another hen
which was heading for the barn.
Whoops!
She tripped over with the egg basket.
Three eggs rolled into a puddle,
two rolled into some mud,
and one rolled under the gate
of the pigsty.

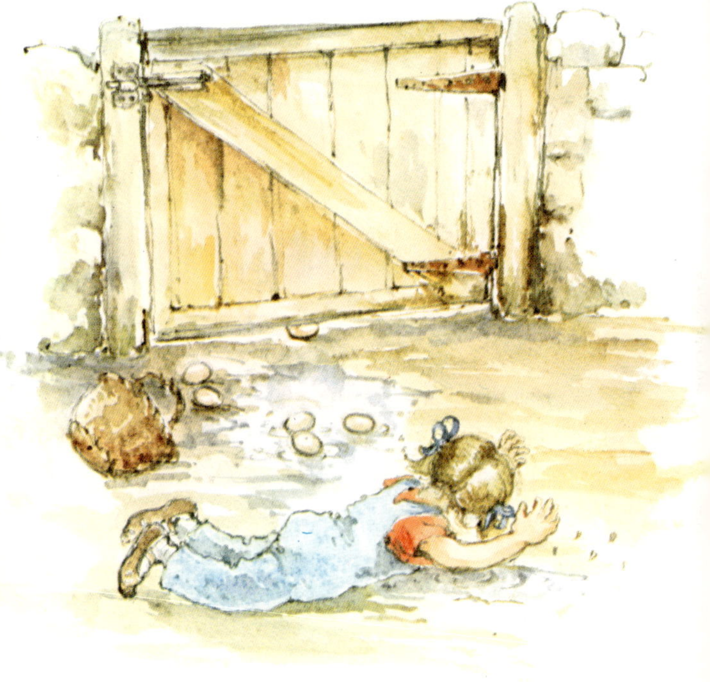

Mary picked up
the five wet and muddy eggs
and then opened the gate
of the pigsty to pick up
the last one.

Two little piglets saw their chance.
They squeezed past Mary to freedom.

They ran across the yard,

under the gate,

around the pond

and towards
the vegetable patch.

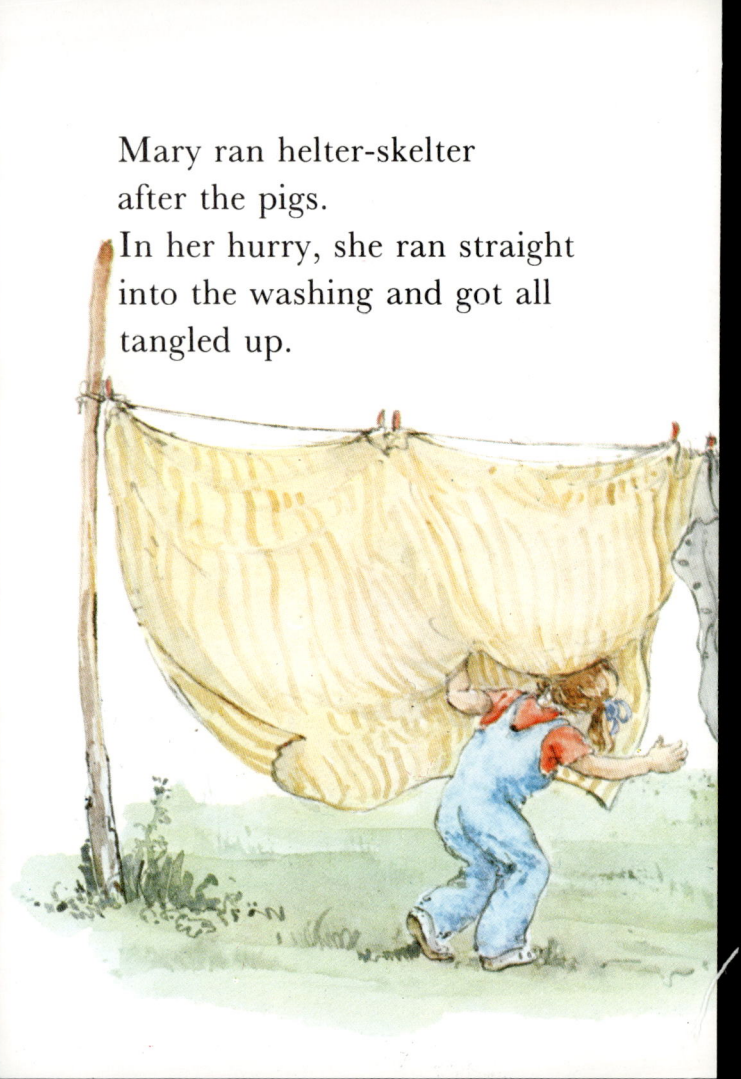

Mary ran helter-skelter
after the pigs.
In her hurry, she ran straight
into the washing and got all
tangled up.

She twisted and turned
and pulled at the sheet.

Suddenly, the old, frayed line snapped and the washing fell all over the grass.

"Bother," said Mary, looking around.

The goat beside her was minding its own business, munching grass.

Mary looked at the goat
and had an idea.
She untied its rope and used it
to mend the washing line.

"That was clever of me," she thought as she hung up the washing.
She didn't think about the goat!

Ian, meanwhile, was still trying
to catch chickens.
Two of them had flown into
the wheatfield.
Ian went through the pasture
to find them.
But he forgot to shut
any of the gates.

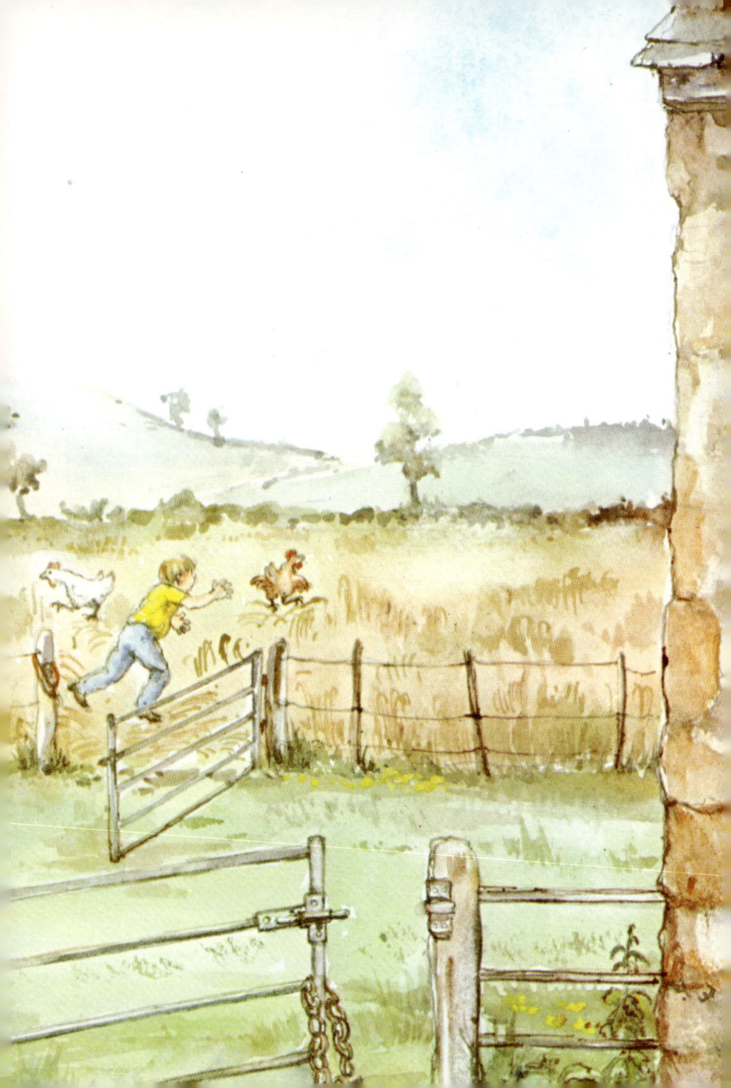

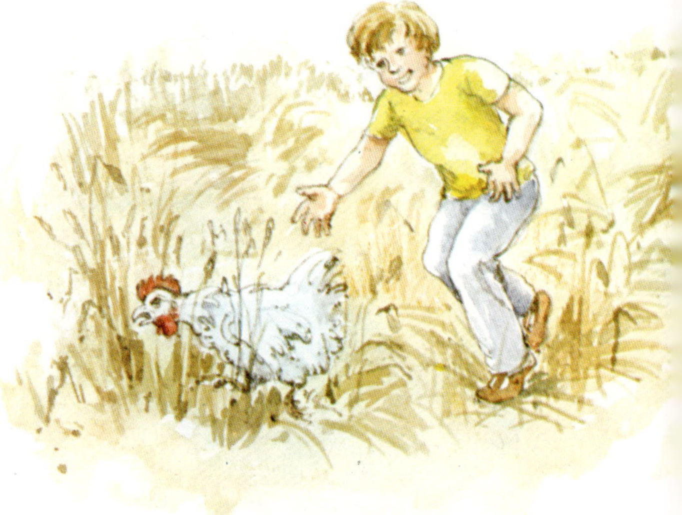

Ian ran this way and that
chasing the hens and trampling
the wheat as he went.

The donkey, seeing that the gate
was open, wandered into the farmyard.
Mary came into the farmyard
just in time to see him
disappear into the barn.
She followed.

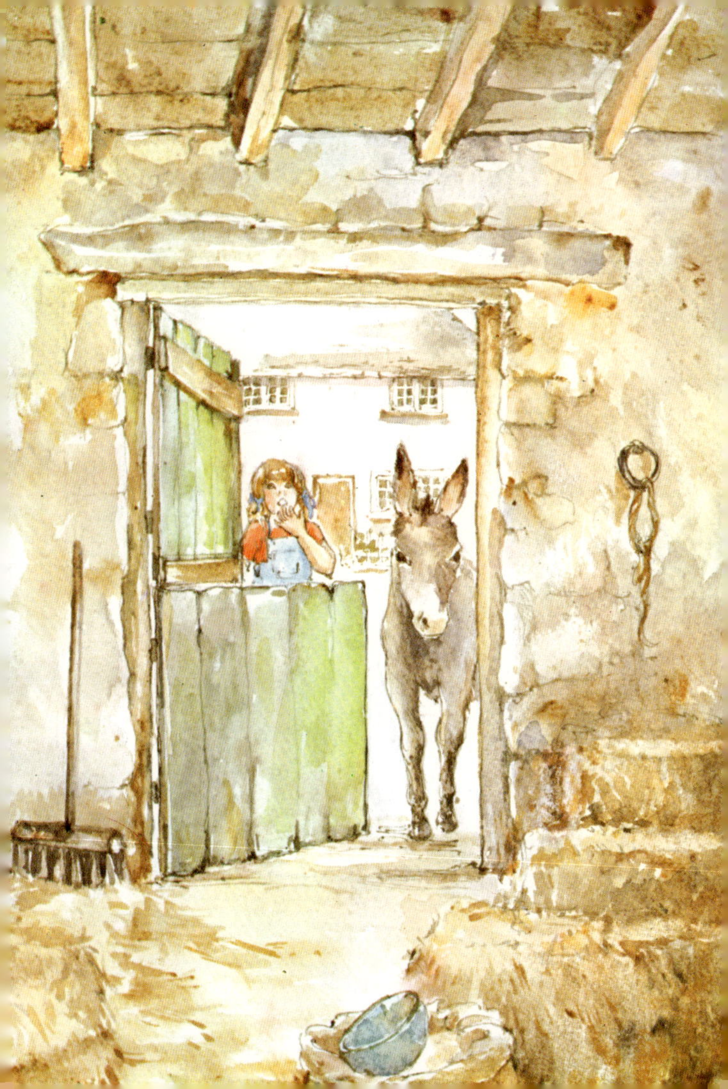

The barn was warm and dark.
Mary peered about looking
for the donkey.
Then she heard a rustling
and a snuffling.
"That's him," she said to herself.
When she went closer,
she heard a tiny mewing
and saw Suzie, the cat,
with four tiny kittens.
They were all curled up
on some old potato sacks.

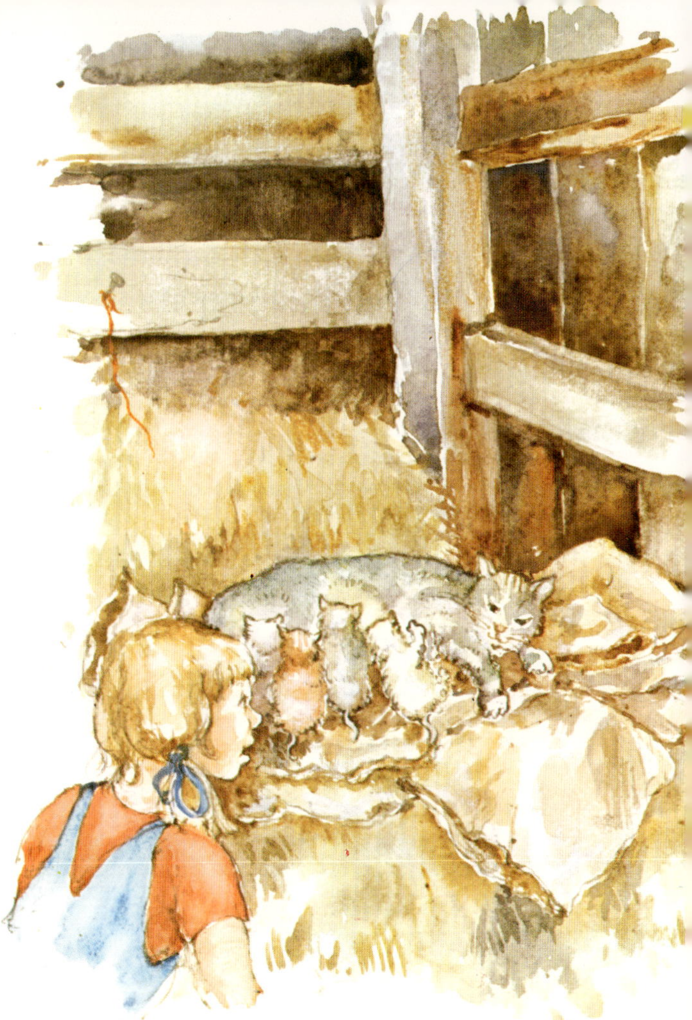

Out of the barn she ran, calling,
"I've found Suzie, I've found her.
Come and see! Come and see!"
Mrs Benn came running to see
what all the noise was about.
She couldn't believe her eyes.

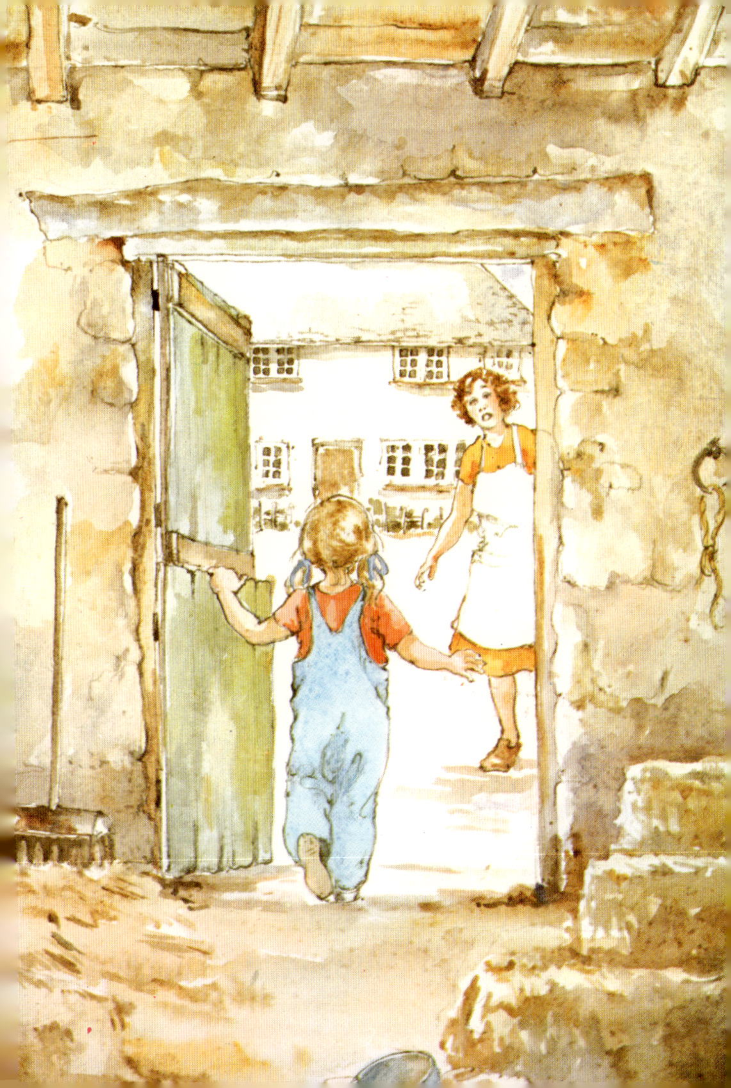

The piglets were in the vegetable patch, digging for tasty roots.

The goat was in the flowerbed,
chewing a mouthful of prize flowers.

The cockerel was on the gatepost, crowing with all his might.

The donkey was in the barn,
munching hay.

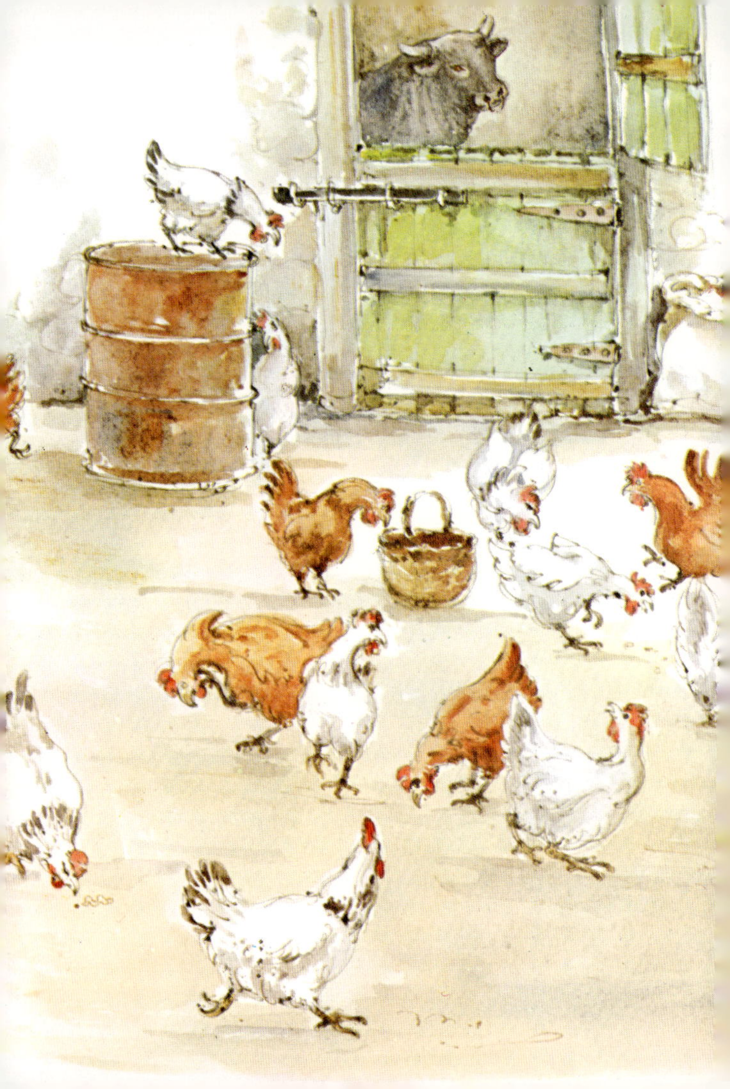

The chickens were all over
the place,
and Ian and Mary were grinning
from ear to ear.
Only the big, black bull
was still safely in his stall.

Mrs Benn opened her mouth
to tell Ian and Mary off.
But before she could say a word,
Mary told her about Suzie.

Mrs Benn was so pleased to hear
the news, she quite forgot
to be cross.

She called everyone to help.
Soon all the animals were back
in their right places
and all the gates firmly shut.

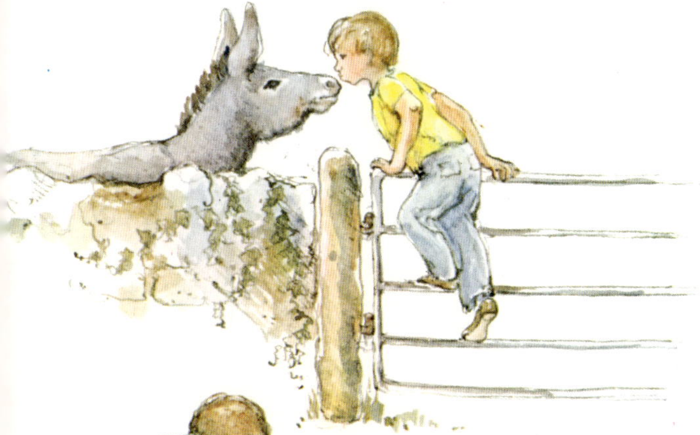

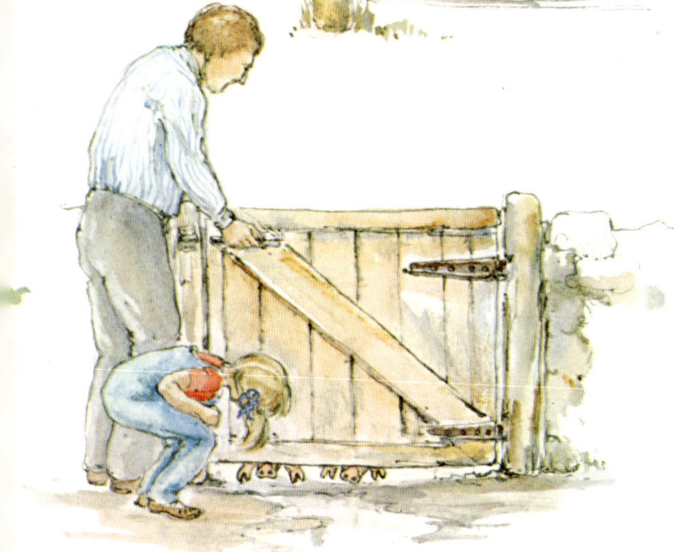

Mrs Benn made Suzie a soft bed.
The four kittens curled up
with Suzie, who purred and purred.
Ian, Mary, Mummy and Daddy
and all the Benns sat down
to an enormous tea of jam
and bread and cakes.
They all agreed it had been
a very busy day indeed.

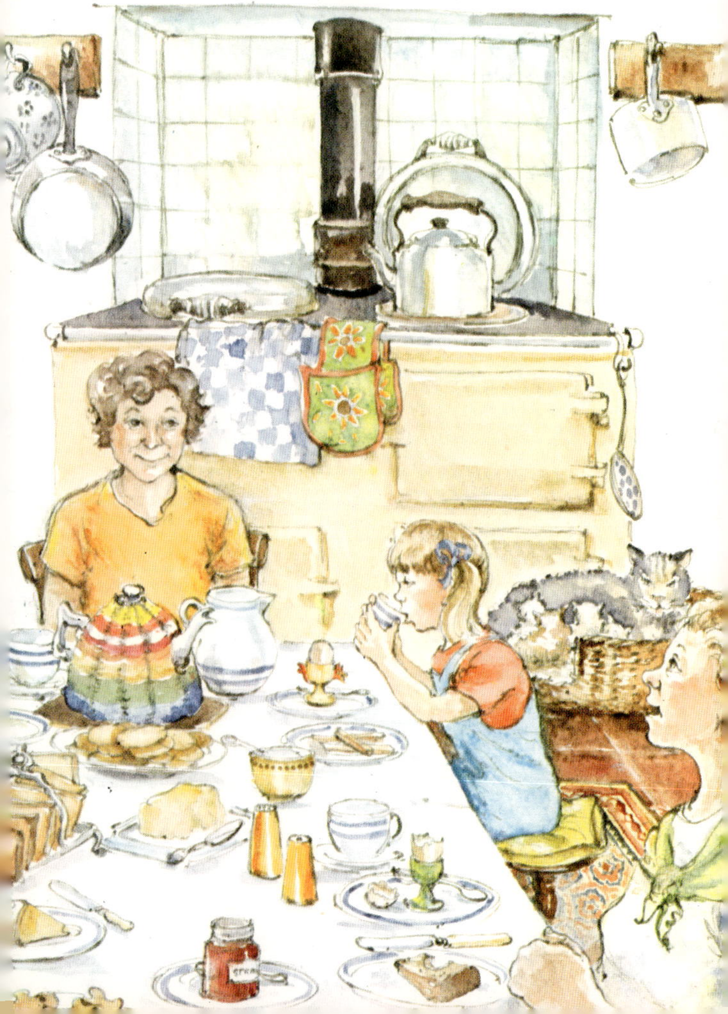

Before they left the farm
Ian and Mary made a promise:

"Next time we go to the country we'll remember to close *all* the gates."

MY HOLIDAY LIBRARY

First Edition Copyright © 1983
Reprinted 1984
The Reader's Digest Association
Limited,
25 Berkeley Square, London W1X 6AB

All rights reserved.

® READER'S DIGEST
is a registered trademark of
The Reader's Digest Association, Inc.
of Pleasantville, New York, U.S.A.

Phototypeset by Tradespools Limited,
Frome, Somerset
Printed in Hong Kong